5 YEARS IN THERAPY!

Acknowledgements

I would like to acknowledge everyone who has influenced my life, whether that be good or bad, as without those characters there would be no book.

To protect the identity of individuals, I have changed the names of people and some of the places.

Disclaimer

If you wish to apply any ideas contained in this book, I will not be held responsible for the outcome. It is therefore understood that you will take full responsibility for your own actions.

Email: catherineerellison@gmail.com

5 YEARS IN THERAPY!

This chapter is taken from my main book, Change or Die: Abuse to Addiction to Abundance. I have made some small alterations so that it stands alone as a short true story describing my five years' experience of psychoanalytic therapy while also training as an integrative psychotherapist.

In this chapter more than any, I have written about some of the techniques I used along with the therapy to improve my own life. If you glean some gems of wisdom and insights from reading this, I will be very happy. Nevertheless, it is not my intention to suggest that any reader follow my examples, as I would not be held responsible for the outcome. Now that I have provided my disclaimer read on.

Although I could see a huge improvement in my behaviour and my ability to deal with situations I also knew I still had a long way to go. I was continuing to struggle with an understanding of my feelings and was limited in my repertoire of coping strategies. As a result, I was referred for psychoanalytic psychotherapy. On receiving my first letter to attend an assessment interview I felt quite anxious. I had read so much about the criteria needed to be accepted as a client. I was concerned that I would not be considered, as my psychology books described the 'YAVIS Syndrome'. This is an acronym that stands for: Young, Attractive, Verbal,

5 YEARS IN THERAPY!

Intelligent, and Successful. Yes, that was the criteria I thought I was expected to fit. And yes, you have guessed, I would have had more chance of finding a one ended stick than fitting that description. I found out later that clients are no longer assessed on that criteria; just as well or this chapter would be missing.

Prior to the assessment I had to fill out some extremely personal questionnaires, which were as sensitive as washing your face with a scrubbing brush. There were a lot of intrusive, probing questions regarding all sorts of abuse. Given these were to be completed in potential clients' own homes without professional support I felt they were extremely thoughtless and inappropriate. Without a doubt they could have caused problems for anyone who was vulnerable. I did make a comment at the end of the questionnaire, as to how inappropriate I thought the questions were. I said that anyone answering these questions without support could be left traumatised. I am aware that there were so many complaints that they were eventually changed. Well done us!

A couple of months later I was given an appointment to see a therapist in the unit. He asked if I would mind being watched through a one-way mirror and listened to through a microphone, which came down through the ceiling. Well yes, I would mind, but could I tell them that? I thought if I said 'No' that they would say I was an unsuitable candidate for the therapy. Listen to the fear of retribution in my response. I just

5 YEARS IN THERAPY!

projected my experience of previous relationships straight onto the therapist with no evaluation of reality. I was asked to attend a total of three assessment interviews which were spread over five months. They told me months later that I had been accepted, and my name would be placed on a waiting list. I could expect to hear from them in about a year and a half, in all I waited just under four years. They obviously weren't in a hurry to see me, probably hoping I would get better or die so that they could strike me off their waiting list.

I arrived for my first session about ten minutes early to give myself time to feel comfortable. Who was I kidding? A woman came down the stairs and called my name. I walked forward, put my hand out, and introduced myself. That went down like a ton of bricks. She gave me a look that said, 'Who do you think you are shaking hands with me? I'm the therapist.' We made fleeting eye contact, before she led the way upstairs to her room. It was a square room, not very tastefully decorated. A picture of a bridge hung on the wall, which obviously was meant to reassure the client of the therapeutic process of crossing over to the other side and feeling better. Of course, unless you had some knowledge of the symbolism of the bridge there was little chance of knowing the therapeutic implications of the picture. It would just look like a meaningless picture, making the observer wonder why someone would choose such a hideous piece of artwork. The room was furnished with three chairs, a desk, filing cabinet,

5 YEARS IN THERAPY!

and large green plant. Behind her seat was some shelving which supported her book collection; of course, each book was clearly related to her work. It would have been far too revealing to have a collection of books which represented her real taste in literature. Her desk was usually littered with paperwork and her briefcase was always placed down by her chair.

At the beginning of the session she did not speak to me, she just sat and looked at me. I can remember feeling the fear of God rising up in my chest area. I started to babble and continued to babble until the end of the session. It was a daunting experience being left in a room alone with her. I began describing my life in some detail, as I understood it at that point. Just prior to the end of the session I made a remark about the chair she had chosen to sit on which was higher than the one for the clients. I asked her if she had an issue with power and needed to represent this in her chair, rather than any 'real' power. That was brave of me wasn't it? At the end of the session I felt as if she had started an operation and cut the centre of my chest open. The second session followed a similar scene. However, I did notice that she was sitting on a chair the same height as my own. I did not dare think that she had made this change because of my remark the previous week. I did find out near the end of my therapy almost six years later that this was the case. At the end of the second session I felt as if she had opened the top of my head up and started to pull out

5 YEARS IN THERAPY!

all the stuff I had buried for years. In the third session I felt as though I walked out with no clothes on. At the beginning of the fourth session I said to her, *"In the first session I felt as though you started an operation and cut my chest open. With the second session I felt as though you had opened the top of my head up and started to pull out all the stuff I had buried. The third session made me feel as if I had walked out with no clothes on. When I work with people I try to put them together before they leave the session, not tear them apart. You are sending me out feeling worse than when I come in."* With her expressionless face she responded with, "This is psychoanalysis." What could I say? If I wanted to continue, I had to take what she offered, which was clearly not quite what I imagined. I had imagined a wonderful, kind, caring therapist who was going to make all my psychological problems disappear. Not a steely eyed bleached blond-haired woman who was making me feel as if I had more problems than I started with.

Nevertheless, I persevered, as I had read so much about the potency of psychoanalysis, I was going to give it my best shot. The first months of therapy were spent with me urgently trying to build a picture in her head of my life. I was terrified of this woman, I would arrive at the session and not be able to breathe for the first five minutes. This was not because I was out of condition and found the stairs too much, but rather that I was having an anxiety attack being in the same room as her. I spent most of my time talking while looking at the ceiling. I was more frightened of her than I was of all the criminals I came across in Newcastle. Every week I would suffer from anxiety at the thought of going to see her. If I felt as though I had upset her during a session I would be in a state of terror for the whole week. I'd expect her to be really nasty when I returned the following week. I would walk into the therapy room and bring the matter back to her attention. I would tentatively explore how she felt, (making her the client hee hee) she just sat with her expressionless, steely eyed face and turned everything I said back on me. She would interpret my feelings towards her as how I felt towards my mother as a child. At first I really didn't understand this. Eventually I could see what was happening, and as the months passed, I began to get in touch with the reality of my childhood feelings. This took a long time, given that I had spent the last thirty odd years from the age of seven repressing them.

I will explain the difference between repressing emotions and suppressing emotions, as I think you might find this helpful. We suppress memories when they are uncomfortable, painful, or we are just unable to face up to or deal with a particular memory. That is, we make a conscious decision to stop thinking about whatever it may be, nevertheless the memories are still held in the conscious mind. Repression on the other hand, is usually the result of very painful, traumatic or distressing emotions or thoughts. When we repress memories,

5 YEARS IN THERAPY!

they are put into the subconscious mind and we have no knowledge of their existence. These memories are more difficult to deal with in therapy, as they are extremely difficult to access. However, they will hugely affect a person's life, their thoughts, feelings and influence all their decisions in an unhealthy way. The person will have no awareness of why this is happening. At some level they will know there is something wrong, but they will not know what it is. For instance, if someone has been beaten with a belt by a teacher as a young child, they may not be able to remember the beatings, but could go into a state of terror when meeting anyone who resembles that particular teacher or anyone holding a belt in their hand.

The brain is a lot more complex and cleverer than we give it credit for, and will use various methods to protect us from trauma. Only thing is, it will usually bring the trauma into our conscious awareness later in life when it feels we are more able to deal with the situation. That is, if we live in an abusive environment our energy is focused on surviving that environment rather than dealing with the abuse. If we are eventually lucky enough to end up in an environment that is loving and supportive the brain begins to feel safe enough to allow the past into the conscious mind. This is in order to deal with what was previously buried in the unconscious. Bit of a bummer that, is it not?

5 YEARS IN THERAPY!

A lot of my early therapy was spent dealing with my completely neurotic thoughts; everything was out of all proportion. If I'd said something to someone, I would play it over and over in my mind, and wonder what the other person would think. Or more to the point, I would imagine there would be repercussions for what I'd said. When I was drinking, I had none of these problems. Yes, that is right, being sober brought a lot more psychological problems than being drunk, that was for sure. When I was drunk, I didn't care what anyone thought about me, as it really didn't matter. Nevertheless, I found I constantly struggled with my emotional and mental health during the first few years of my sobriety.

It took a long time to stop the overreactions I was having to various situations. For instance, I would find I was really distressed about something which had happened. Then in the therapy sessions I would be able to explain what was going on in my mind and eventually access the root cause of the problem. Your right in thinking it would normally be traced to some childhood event which I had not dealt with. It would then be dealt with on the emotional and intellectual level, after which the neurosis would disappear. That sounds simple, believe me it was far from simple. It often took months to deal with the repressed emotions of a particular situation.

One day during the therapy I accessed a particularly traumatic memory which left me unable to speak. At the time I

5 YEARS IN THERAPY!

was doing a degree in Psychology with the Open University and ran the self-help sessions for our group. When the other students were ringing me up, I could only stutter. The beginning of words would repeat rapidly before I could complete the whole word. Trying to complete a full sentence was out of the question. This was a tough time; I felt so vulnerable and avoided speaking on the telephone or having conversations. That was a first! In all fairness I was very worried, as I did not know if I was ever going to be able to speak properly again. That would have ruined my public speaking career!

I think the therapist was also scared; I could see the fear in her face when I arrived at the sessions. Of course, psychoanalysts don't take any responsibility for problems which might arise during the therapy. No, that would be my mother's fault, even if she had been dead for twenty years. Nevertheless, weeks later my stuttering stopped as quickly as it started, much to my delight.

Given I was experiencing so many problems with the psychotherapy itself, you might be wondering why I kept going to the sessions. It was a bit odd, but I knew at some level that this woman was triggering issues from my past that really needed to be dealt with if I was to be free of my baggage from the past. During our encounters I was being pivoted back through time, to those childhood experiences with my mother.

5 YEARS IN THERAPY!

Now that is what they call transference in the world of counselling and psychotherapy. We all experience transference in different relationships, but just for those who are unsure of the meaning of this word I will provide a simple explanation. Transference is the transferring of feeling from an earlier relationship of an important person, such as a mother, onto a new relationship. Now my therapist provided the ideal environment for transference, as she acted as a blank slate. That is, she would just sit and allow me to project all my feelings, fears and fantasies onto her. This gave me the space I needed to deal with my past.

After starting the therapy, I began to realise that my thoughts about myself were very negative. That is, my internal dialogue would go something like: You are useless, stupid, worthless and on it went. I had clearly internalized all the negativity from my childhood and relationships to date. That is, their way of thinking about me had become mine. I read a book about *The Power of Positive Thinking* by *Norman Vincent Peale*. After reading the book I decided I was never going to say a bad word about myself again. You know what happens when I decide to do something. I do it! I started to monitor my thoughts; and every time I thought something negative about myself, I changed it to something positive. It was a bit like learning how to drive a car - at first, I had to think about what I was doing and eventually it just became automatic.

5 YEARS IN THERAPY!

This really helped when people came to me and said they had low self-esteem; I would ask them what their self-talk was like in their heads. Inevitably they would say things like, I tell myself I am stupid, ugly, fat, useless, a failure and so on. I would ask how they would feel if someone else called them these names. The answer would usually be, "I would feel devastated, angry or hurt." I would go on to point out that it did not matter whether we said these things to ourselves, or other people said them, it would have the same impact. That is, this destructive way of talking to ourselves would destroy our self-esteem and confidence. I would ask, "If you had a child and you wanted it to grow up confident and self-assured how would you treat it?" Most people would know the formula required to produce such a wonderful human being. They would reply, "I would love, praise and encourage my child. I would not criticise, berate or put my child down." Exactly, well why don't you treat yourself as though you are the most precious child in the world? That is, you do a reparenting job on yourself and this time give yourself all the love, gentleness, encouragement and praise to build your own self-esteem. Believe me this way of thinking actually works wonders.

As trust was developing in the therapy I was ending up in full-blown regressions on a weekly basis. It was as though my adult self was taking my inner child to the sessions, and when I got there, there was no adult self to talk to the therapist. During the regressions I would have the intellect of whatever age I had regressed to. In hindsight I found this whole process fascinating. For example, if I regressed to the age of a three-year-old, I would also have the intellectual understanding, the language and voice of a three-year-old. The dialogue of a three-year-old is quite distinctive, for instance they might say, 'Me frightened.' rather than, 'I'm frightened.' I was becoming quite a master at recognising the age I had regressed to, by identifying the grammatical structure of the language I used during the regressions. What I found amazing about the regressions was that the time was not experienced as the actual time in the session. That is, when the therapist called time, (a bit like the bar staff when I was drinking), I would argue that it couldn't possibly be time; I had only been in the session for a few minutes. I found it fascinating that the regressed state I was experiencing not only took me back to a reliving of a particular event, but that it also took me from the 'real' time I was experiencing during the session.

As I journeyed through my therapy, I started to understand why I was so emotionally stunted. Although saying that, I had no concept of ever being emotionally stunted until I started therapy, I just thought I was perfectly normal, as you do! I was soon to learn that with an addictive personality where the attention is focused on the object of the addiction, it was not possible to invest in my own emotional growth. Now I am going to explain this further, not that I think you want to train as a psychotherapist, but because I hope you will find all this

5 YEARS IN THERAPY!

very interesting. If we take any form of addictive behaviour, of which there are too many to mention here, but whether it be: eating disorders, drug or alcohol addiction, workaholic, co-dependent relationships, social media, gambling, exercise or religion the person's thoughts are constantly focused on the object of their addiction. The energy is seldom used to look inward. We can only grow and learn about ourselves if we take the time to get to know ourselves, and how the world is impacting us. If we look at all the great spiritual gurus who ever lived, one of the main things they all had in common would be that they spent time alone meditating and reflecting on life. That is, they understood themselves and their emotions. I have met many highly intelligent professional people who are geniuses in their field of work, yet they lack self-awareness. This is often a result of all their energy being focused obsessively on their work, rather than their own emotional growth.

I am not suggesting that everyone should take a course in meditation or sit in the desert for 40 days fasting to get to know themselves. In fact, a friend of mine joined a Buddhist Monastery and started to meditate three times a day for two hours each time. No one told her how dangerous this could be. Meditation can and usually will have the same results as psychotherapy, in that all the repressed memories will begin to surface during the meditation. She was on the verge of a complete breakdown and could not cope with the memories which were now surfacing. So, we see that even though meditation, just like psychotherapy can be useful, it also has to be treated with respect. That is, it has to be done sensibly with experienced, knowledgeable guides.

Over the years I watched thousands of my clients change their lives through counselling and psychotherapy; it provided them with the space and the tools to make the changes. It also never failed to surprise me when people came through my door and said. "I've been good all my life; I'm a good person or a good Christian." What they meant by this was - they were a doormat for other people to abuse and misuse because they put everyone before themselves. They deviated from any form of honest straight forward communication, as this would upset the other person. If they mentioned being a Christian, which they often did, I would ask, "Is Jesus good?" After a few seconds thought the response would be, "Oh yes, Jesus is good." I would follow through with, "Did you know that Jesus was one of the most straight forward, straight talking people who ever lived? He didn't pull his punches and said it how it was. In other words, he was honest and never put up with inappropriate behavior." For some reason we are conditioned to keep putting the feelings of others before our own, at a great cost to our own psychological wellbeing. People often muddle up being good with putting up with insults and abuse. They would say, "I don't want to hurt their feelings if I tell them what I think." I'd say, "In other words, let them get away with upsetting you and hurting your feelings while you continue with your dishonest relationship allowing yourself to be abused." Well this was certainly something I'd stopped doing, and fortunately many of the people I came into contact with followed suit. That is, they started to understand the importance of attending to their own needs before succumbing to everyone else's. As a result they developed a far more honest way of communicating.

Better get back to telling you about my own therapy. Not long after starting I felt as though I had a huge black pool of mud in my chest, it was like a constant dull ache. I mentioned in an earlier chapter that my head felt like a pressure cooker, steaming away. Both these feelings went on for years while I was having therapy before eventually disappearing. Now I have no real psychological explanation for the constant discomfort I felt in my body during this period, but would go so far as to say I believe it was a result of the undealt with emotions. I drew this conclusion because, as I worked through the baggage I was carrying, it was like a massive weight being lifted. I felt so much better and free from the torment that had gone on for so long.

Now no chapter on psychoanalysis would be complete without the mention of love. Yes, after getting sober I kept falling in love. I didn't know I hadn't been in love until I fell in love properly. I say properly, but it really wasn't, it was

5 YEARS IN THERAPY!

what many of us experience as falling in love, but it is a very unhealthy, immature falling in love. That is, it was the experience of thinking constantly about the other person, where the relationship was more in my head than reality. This is the same as the addictive behaviour I mentioned earlier. It takes the persons thoughts away from themselves to focus their energy on the object of wherever their love is directed. Before this I thought that love was 'in my eye' and that is just how it was. I must say that my eyesight must have been terribly poor given the 'clips' I chose for partners. I should have gone to Specsavers. I was now falling "in love" with people who I perceived as intellectually superior, although I did not realise this at the time. I did not think, 'Oh there's a bright spark I will just fall in love with them.' No, there just seemed no rhyme nor reason for what I was experiencing. I had no idea why I fell in love at that time nor why I chose the person I did to fall in love with.

I certainly had a lot to learn; you know when everything the other person does is a sign of their love for you and you tell your friends, 'I saw him wink at me.' Not that he had a piece of dust in his eye. 'He was smiling at me, when I was in the audience at the conference.' Yes, and another two hundred people. The whole world could be falling apart, and it wouldn't matter; the only thing that mattered was the object of my love. This was an education, a very painful education I may add and certainly one I would have been happy to do

5 YEARS IN THERAPY!

without. I went through this state of affairs several times, and I must say the emotional pain I felt was excruciating. There was also the other side of this coin, as the process of falling in love is the highest high a person can experience; apparently it is even higher than taking ecstasy. I think for a while I was getting addicted to the highs created by falling in love. Does that make sense as it did to me at the time? After a while I started to realise that I was being taken to new heights, as I was going through these experiences. It took several years, but I eventually got to a place where I stopped 'falling in love'. And no, this was not a result of becoming bitter, twisted and hating the human race. It was a result of reaching a level of psychological maturity with the combination of my spiritual experience and therapy that made me a lot more comfortable in myself.

The therapy really helped me to move forward intellectually too, which was a phenomenon I least expected. Before you begin to wonder how I could possibly become more intelligent, given intelligence is often considered reasonably stable from the cradle to the grave, I will explain this. Most people do not realise that the brain uses more energy than any other organ in the body. A massive amounts of my energy was being used to keep my repressed memories out of my conscious awareness. As the repressed memories were being released with the therapy, my energy was no longer needed to keep them in my unconscious mind. I could actually feel my brain taking quantum leaps, this was an amazing bonus from the therapy. I could feel my ability to think clearer and solve problems improve. I was free to use my energy now, not only to improve my life, but I also felt as though I was academically more able than I'd ever been. For the first time in my life I was becoming free from the shackles of my past. I was also beginning to stop repeating the constant steam of chaos from the past.

Therapy was now providing me with the opportunity to tell someone what I felt and workout why I felt it. That certainly put my brain into overdrive. I did feel self-indulgent; a whole hour a week just for me from someone who gave me their undivided attention, with the whole purpose of helping me to improve my life. I did not only spend one hour a week in the therapy, I made sure that almost every night I put at least an hour aside to work through the material I had brought up during the sessions. This hour was probably the most productive hour of the day, given the amount of pain, hurt, anger and rage I was able to deal with outside of the therapy. I had no idea I'd buried so many feelings over the years.

Although after getting sober I had started to slowly become aware of many feelings, during the therapy even more feelings were evolving. My brain seemed to be going through a slow defrosting, I know that might sound a bit crazy, but it is how it felt. As my feelings were coming into being I was beginning to

5 YEARS IN THERAPY!

be able to identify and make sense of them. I found this a really peculiar experience, as I was so disconnected from myself.

As I was getting stronger, and my confidence was growing I stopped tolerating people who I found abusive or inappropriate. If I felt someone was being inappropriate, I would say, "I find you insulting, abusive or whatever." But one thing was for sure I would no longer put up with anyone who I felt would damage me in any way. I once told a friend who was complaining about some of the friends she had around her. "Why don't you score people on a scale of 1 to 10 and if they fall below 5, three times, knock them off your party list." Now I know that might sound harsh, and completely understand that when our friends hit difficult times they need a lot more support from those around them. In those circumstances doing this would not be justified. However, many people foster friendships with people who are pulling them down and needy all the time. In cases like this I think the method I described works wonders. I am also aware that some people like to have this sort of friend, as it makes them feel needed. If that is the case continue as you are, but at least be aware that you are choosing to have friends who are full of doom and gloom and will drag you down. Occasionally I meet someone who wants to play the martyr and tell me, or rather bore the pants of me, telling me all the woes of their other friends. I usually just make it clear that I am not the slightest bit interested and would rather go home and watch a good film than listen to a load of doom and gloom about someone I don't even know. I imagine most of us feel this way, when someone is going on about someone's problems who we have never met, but think most people are too polite to ask them to change the subject. I've wasted enough of my precious time in this life time and believe by telling the person what I think helps to improve their social skills! A bit of tact does come in useful here.

One thing is for sure I no longer chose to have a load of negative people in my life. I am now very selective of the calibre of friends I spend my time with. I was now also improving my ability to assess a person's personality quite early in the relationship. If I found they started with the off handed put downs, negative remarks, or calling people names, I quickly put a stop to the relationship. This would be best understood with a story about a friend who told me she was being bullied at work. We discussed how she could handle these situations in the immediacy of them happening. She came back and said things had improved, but would it be all right if she allowed them to go so far before tackling the situation. My response was a resounding, "No, if you do that where do you draw the line?" If someone is being inappropriate or abusive it is important to address it in the here and now, or as soon as possible afterwards. I found that if I did not deal with inappropriate behaviour in a healthy manner I would become resentful. I also believed that if I did not respect myself then no one else would. When I was in the rehab this is a skill, I really did master. We were encouraged to say if there was anything which we were uncomfortable with. If there was anything going on in my head that did not feel right, I learned to address it. Sometimes it would amount to something, other times it would be a misunderstanding. One thing was certain, once it was addressed, it no longer messed with my mind. When issues aren't addressed, they will always fester. We have probably all experienced that internal dialogue going; I should have said this or that. It is not worth the hassle; when all this can be prevented by just asking the other person what they meant by what they said or did. At least that way they will either say, "Yes I meant that" or "No there is a misunderstanding." Whenever I checked out my understanding if I felt uncomfortable or confused, I certainly left the situation a lot happier than if I had not checked it out.

Another technique which I used, and if appropriate went on to show numerous other people how to use, was 'The Page in my Diary'. I would ask if they wanted to know about the page in my diary and without fail they would say, "Yes." So, I would tell them, "Every diary has a 'notes page', so every January I would write a list of the things I wanted to change down the side of the page. Along the top of the same page I would write the numbers between 1 and 10. For each issue down the side I would score it where I felt I was, and where I wanted to be. So, for instance, 'being more patient' I might have scored it a four and the goal was to make it an eight. I'd hate to be too patient! It would therefore be scored under the number four and under the number eight.

I would do this right down the list, and for the first few years my page was full of things I wanted to change. That is because I had such a lot of things I felt I had to work on to get to where I wanted to be. Also, the further apart the numbers the lower the self-esteem. I can assure you mine was very low when I first started to do this. I would put all sorts of things on this page like; improve my speaking, confidence, remember birthdays, learn something every day, stop swearing and so on. During the year I would frequently look at the list to check how I was doing. Each January I would write a new list; some things stayed from the previous year, and some dropped off if I had reached my goal. The new list also gave me the opportunity to add new things. As the years continued, I found my list was gradually getting smaller, and eventually I had nothing to put on the list. This was because I was absolutely perfect! This never failed to get a laugh, but it certainly was a brilliant way to have an image of the sort of person I wanted to be and keep track of how I was working towards the image. A lot of people who I know used this method and had great results.

5 YEARS IN THERAPY!

Just in case you hadn't realised I was finding the therapy really helpful. I now had coping skills to deal with difficult situations and could work out the possible consequences of my actions more accurately. I had gained insight into why I kept going into more and more chaos. That did not stop me at that point, however, at least I knew why I kept repeating the behaviour. I was making sense of how my adult life was replicating my childhood. It was as though I was a massive jigsaw and I was beginning to put the pieces into place. Or metaphorically I was slowly making my way up a mountain and the view was growing as I climbed. There was not a therapy available which I did not try over the years after getting sober. Between counselling, thought field, tapping, spiritual healing, voice movement, shen, body massage, Chinese medicine, hypnotherapy, acupuncture, reiki, cupping, you name it and I'd tried it. Most of these therapies played a part in my journey of recovery, as did quite a lot of the people who I met during that period.

I worked on lots of issues during this period of psychoanalysis, as although my therapist would have benefitted from a lesson in social skills, she was what I needed. She was predictable, strong, gentle and had clear boundaries. She didn't flinch when I got angry. I once said to her, "When I die you will put my therapy notes into that filing cabinet and forget that I existed." She responded with, "And what would that feel like?" I just wanted her to say that she cared a dot. This was never to happen, as psychoanalysts would never allow themselves to tell you what they felt. That would be a cardinal sin and worthy of immediate termination of employment.

Nevertheless, there was one day when she actually lost it, and I know this is hard to believe because that is certainly not what psychotherapists are supposed to do. She shouted at me and was really quite aggressive; I was mortified and cut to the bone, here was the one person in the world who I had put my trust into and she had betrayed my trust with her outburst. I left the session with a lump in my throat, but made sure she did not know what I felt. I was so taken aback I could not even respond and just pretended everything was fine. I am also very aware that when I get kicked I certainly do not go belly up with the enemy!

I told myself I was not going to go back to see the wicked witch I would look for another therapist a nice therapist. Me being me I went through the therapists in the yellow pages and picked the best. The one with the PhD who had studied at one of the best universities in the world. Yes she will do. I phoned her up and told her what had happened with my other therapist. She responded with, "O you poor dear" I felt sick you know that, lets stick two fingers down my throat image. Well that is the criteria she met. There was no way I could have someone like that as a therapist. She was sickly nice, no I will just stay

5 YEARS IN THERAPY!

with my nasty therapist, she is perfect for my therapy. Now Catherine is that a bit of transference? Think it could be.

Well now when I went to my next session, she knew fine well she had overstepped her mark. She even looked guilty and once again but believe it or not she actually apologised. Yes she said she was very sorry and should not have lost her temper. She also said, "Does what I did wipe out everything that has gone before?" Now that is quite a deep and meaningful statement which I did need some time to think about. I let her off and forgave her.

On a few occasions I wanted to discuss what I felt were problems with the venue, dates or times of sessions. There was no way that this woman would engage in a conversation; she would analyse my questions. I can't begin to explain how frustrating this was. I would lose my temper and say to her. "Will you just respond to the question?" She would respond with, "You sound angry." That is Psychoanalysis!

Thank you so much for your time and for sharing my journey.

Can I ask if you have found this book useful would you mind leaving a review please? You see, if a book is well reviewed this proves its credibility and helps other readers to know if it is right for them. I also think there is a lot of really good information which could help other people through their journey. Keep safe Catherine Ellison

5 YEARS IN THERAPY!